A Hundred and One Uses of a

DEAD·CAT

SIMON BOND

Methuen
11. New Fetter Lane
London E.C.4

First published in 1981 by
Eyre Methuen Ltd
Reprinted thirteen times 1981
Reprinted 1982 twice by
Methuen London Ltd
11 New Fetter Lane, London EC4P 4EE

Copyright © Simon Bond 1981

ISBN 0 413 48610 9

Printed in Great Britain by
Whitstable Litho Ltd,
Whitstable, Kent

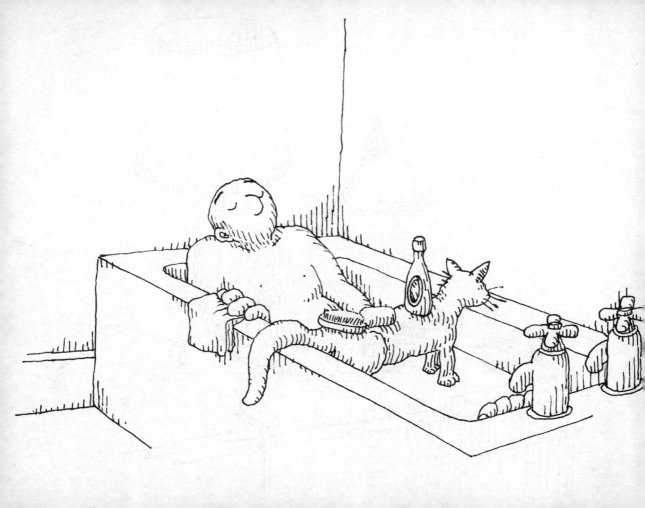

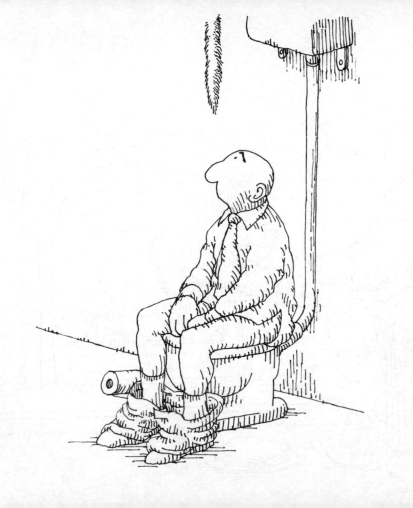

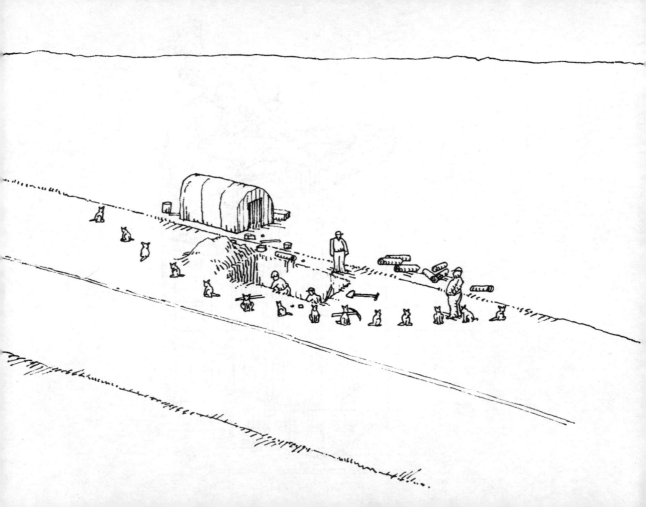

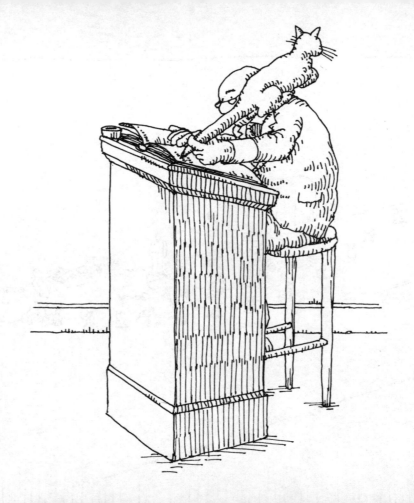

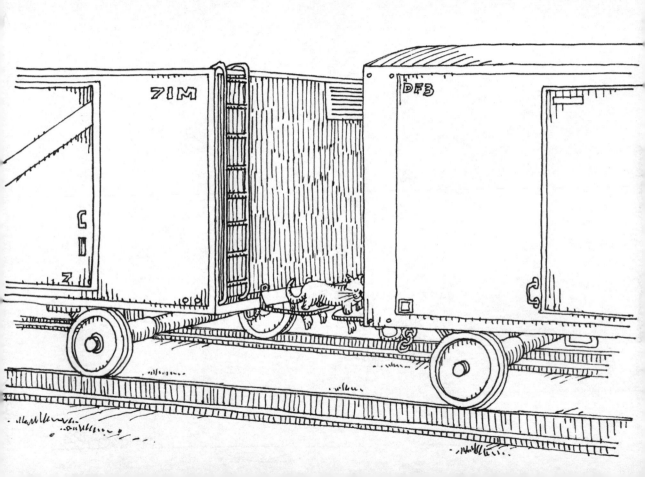

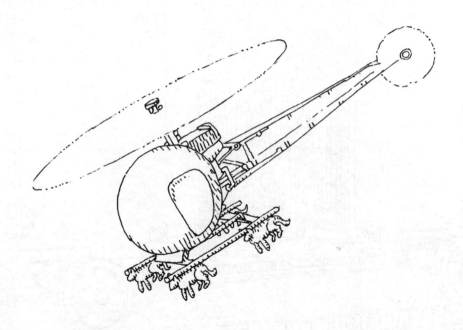

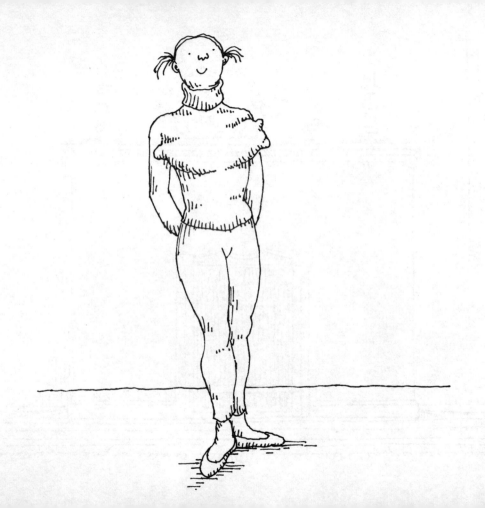

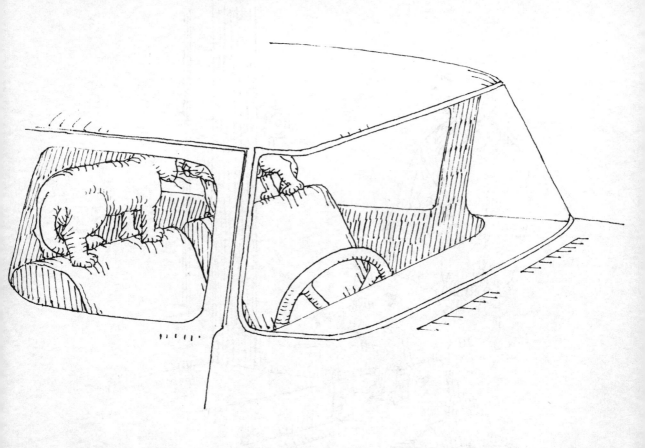

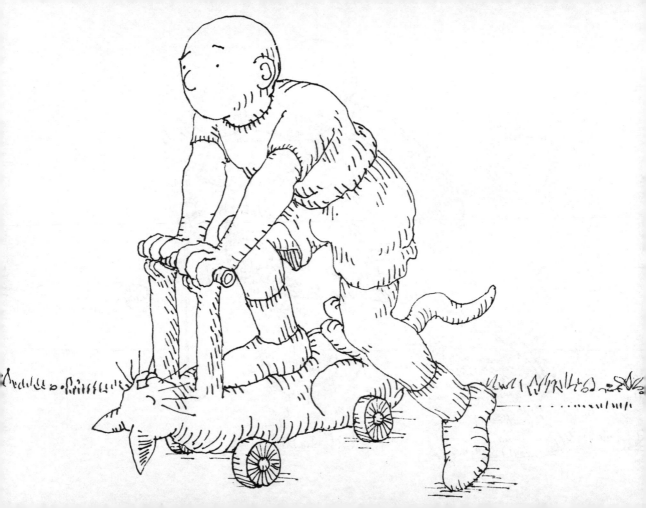

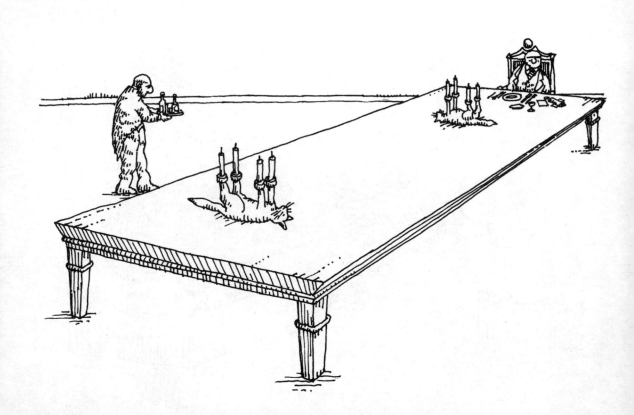

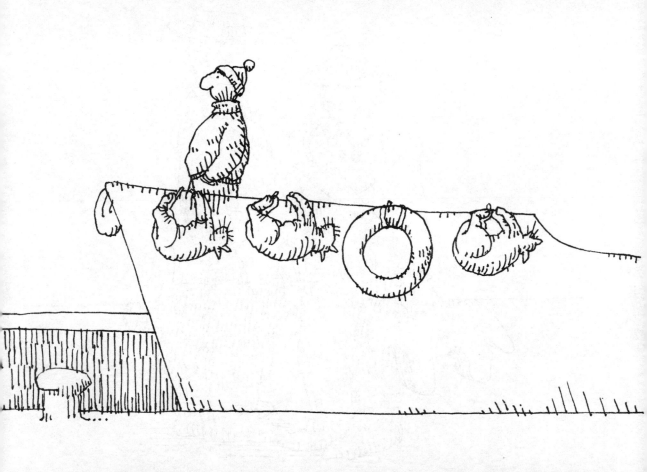

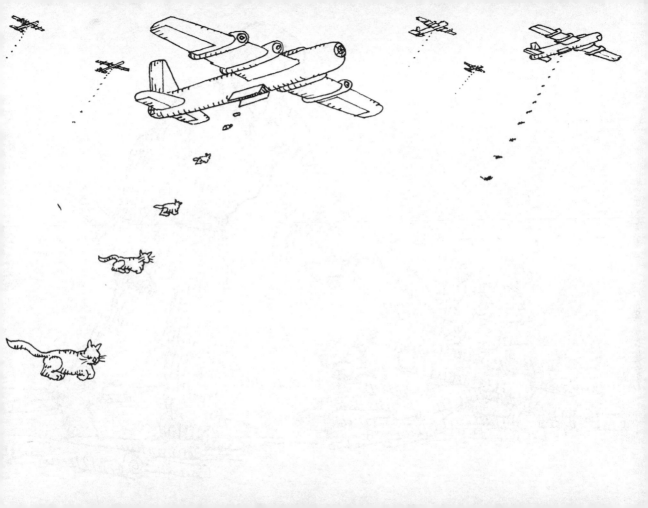

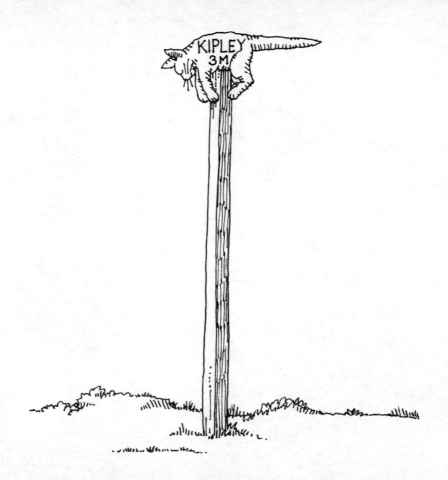

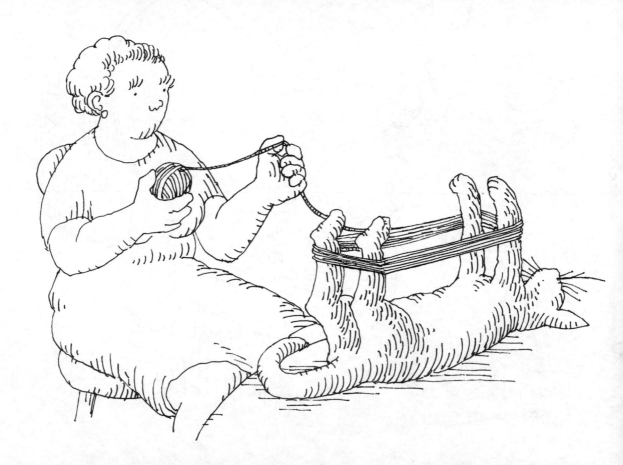

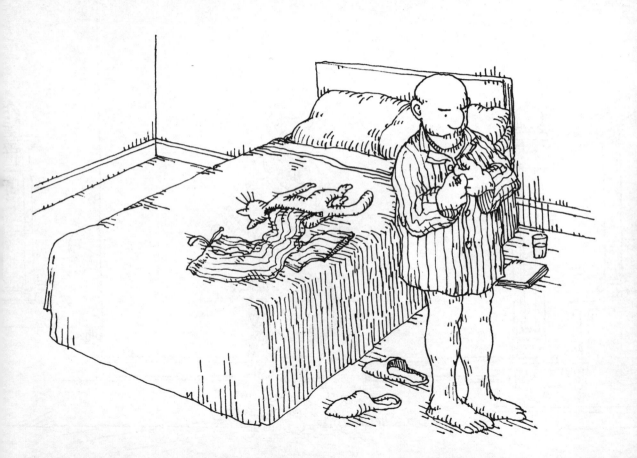

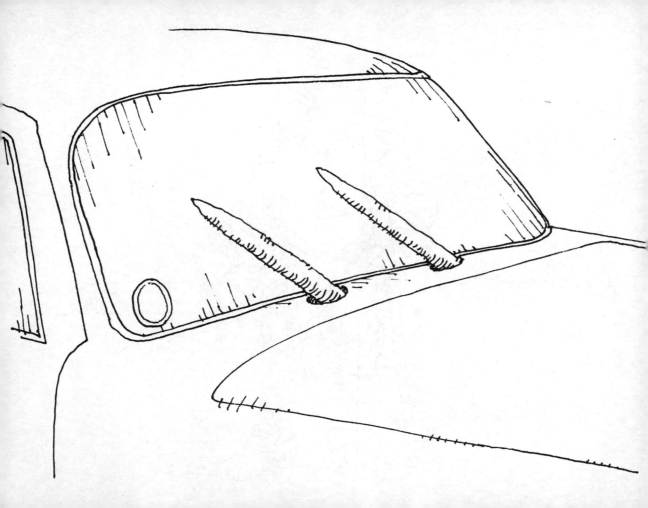

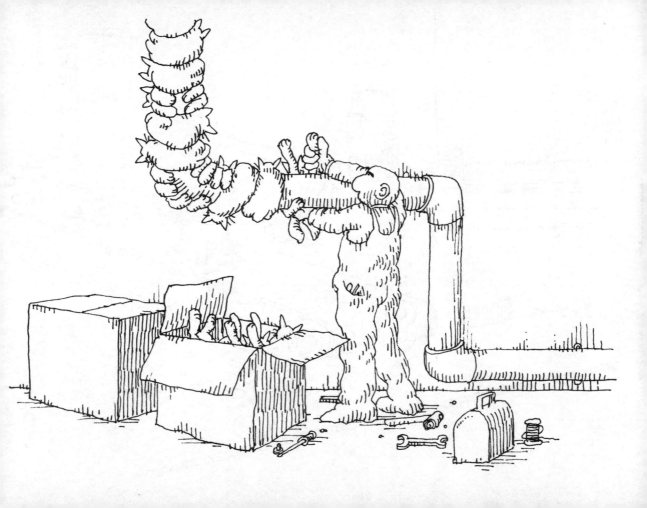

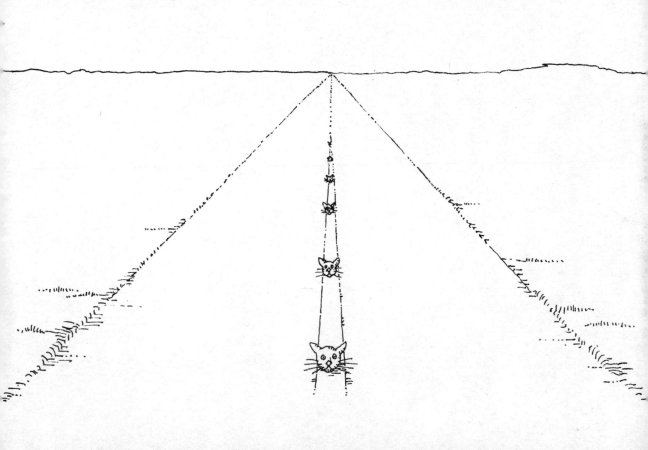